Love Notes On My Windshield

hopelessly unromantic

Desirae Vandam

BookLeaf Publishing

India | USA | UK

Made with ❤ on the BookLeaf Publishing Platform
www.bookleafpub.in
www.bookleafpub.com

Dedication

to the ones who deserve peace

and the ones who love deeper than most

Preface

poems on love and love lost. we love too quickly and unlove too slowly. emotions are meant to be felt, whether through tears, through writing, through art, or through screaming at the top of your lungs into the abyss. if anyone has broken your sweet heart, feel with me. if anyone has ever written notes on your windshield, cry with me. if you've ever been made to feel like a convenience, scream with me.

Acknowledgements

thank you so much to bookleaf for making this possible and so easy.

thank you so the heartbreaking parts of my short life.

thank you to the beauty that has also graced my short life.

thank you to divorce.

thank you to marriage.

thank you to therapy.

thank you to emotion and feeling.

thank you to you.

pt. 1

i need you more than you need me
a necessary part of my reality
salt to the sea
wind to the trees
i need you more than you need me

i need you more than you need me
a necessary part you never did see
water to my seeds
smoke to my flame, my gleam
i need you more than you need me

yes

for you
it will always be yes
even when my heart
does truly want rest
even when no
seems better expressed
for you
it will *always*
be yes

speaking of the weather

maybe you are chaos
and maybe I am peace
maybe you are a blistering summer sun relentlessly
glowing on the desert
and I a brisk and sharp autumn breeze come before the
icy winter
and though we may form tornadoes
quick and surprising, intense and destructive
the tranquil subtleties are what we crave
a gentle, understated peace, evoking a sense of harmony
and all of this that keeps us coming back for the warmth
we find within *this* embrace

concerto in j minor

live music
private studio
tickets sold out
you're the only one that shows

i sing for days
broken record
cat scratches, chalkboard
but to you
a songbird

teethy grin, mouth full
grab my hand
a sudden pull
dance, like falling
quick sand

mouth meets mouth
"how do you do?"
"better now"
falling tower
lean *right into you*

navy blues

one of the best moments
is when you catch me admiring you
just your face
the stubble on your chin
the scar below your eye
you think i haven't noticed
but there's a touch of grey in that eye
your demeanor is so silly
but you're unapologetically you
you're gentle and you're humble
you're powerful, you're... blue
blue is my favorite color and
it's all i see in you
it's bright and soft and comforting
from peace and into sorrow
it's unexpected.. it's *you*
all my favorite things, you are
the sky, the rain... *your eyes*
like an ocean, yeah i guess,
but has the ocean seen..
your eyes..

7. paradise

okay but i think paradise
is just... your favorite oversized sweater
a cozy, crocheted blanket
hiding from stormy weather

the quiet of the evening, sun low and sleeping
when traffic has grown peaceful
the silence that the moonlight brings
a chamomile tea, bedside table

the dimly lit lamp
dust collected and somber
the warmth i lay in, your arms
make the restful night even calmer

if you ask me, i think paradise
might just be breathlessness
the way that it feels, the feeling
when you take the breath straight from my lips

melting right into you
the honey in my tea
closer and closer
melt right into me

paradise is, if you ask me
a tire swing hung from a tree
a flowing dress engulfed in breeze
hand to my cheek, mind at ease

if you ask me where i'd go
to find this place, my paradise
i'd take a few steps back, running start
and dive head first directly into your eyes

8. cups of j

i recognize you
i've seen you before
from every page turn
behind every door

your face, seen in visions
i know how you taste
i've seen you before
i know your embrace

like the smell of warm coffee
i've smelt you before
the comfort just the smell brings
a desire for so much more

love carved

sitting here and i ponder
why the hell can't love just be
just a silly little note
or a carving on a tree
as simple as a wish
a tuft of dandelion carries
off into the wind
but the ground beneath it, buries
deep into the ground
the little wish just starts to sink
and once that wish is gone
it makes us really start to think
maybe another note
could sound a little better
or we'd run into an expert
an incredible woodworker
something could be better
but my love for you will always be
more than just a little love note
or a carving on a tree

redo

if it helped your tomorrow
i'd go back in time
i'd fix every problem
rewrite every rhyme

i'd redo conversations
we had under moon shine
i'd make them so much better
if it meant you might be mine

if happiness came in a box
that store sure would be thriving
i'd be there every day, unable to eat but
every box, for you i would be buying

if lovers in wars
waited weeks for a note
but you can't even type out some words
well, i must be a joke

what's no joke at all
is the way your eyes shine
so much brighter than stars
as you stare right into mine

obsessed with you, no
obsession sounds wrong
but *for you?* for you
i'd dedicate every single love song

but i know you wouldn't sing along

gallery

a hallway, once barren
you fill with frames
bright, expressive art
you bring books, turn each page

every sketch, carbon, graphite
you learn every stroke
pushing all the right ways
planting trees, nurture seeds

sown, watered, roots establish
longing for sun
no grey in sight, you look out well
removing clouds, every last one

protection, not begged for but given
generous to a fault
just a part of your nature
kindness, *love,* your default

love letters on my windshield

i don't believe in liking things
it never seems enough
i never really like things, simply stated
like is just *never* enough

i don't like the sun, it's golden waters
washing us from so far
i don't like the clouds, they're moving in
painting the sky over every star

i don't like the rain because it reminds me of you
as i lay in the cold, coated grass
memories adding sparkling speckles to my face
and the entire sky reminds me too, the deep blue
comforting mass

i don't like that restaurant we went to
i think you know the one
i don't like the love letter you left
on my windshield, it shines more brightly in the sun

i don't like the scar below your right eye
the way you can't grow a full beard

i don't like the way you're so expressive
about all of your deepest loves and fears

i don't like the way your smile turns
when i start a false quarrel about a little thing
i know you know way more than me
i just don't like the passion that you allow to be seen

i don't really like car rides through the park
the ones we used to meet
i don't like how it brought us to this place we are
the place where you cook dinners for me

i don't like the trees, the greens of spring
even though when you didn't like me, they turned
orange
things you've done and said to me in fall
always replay, picked out of storage

i really don't like the way you held me
the one night i left so late, so tired
you tried to get me to stay, i know
but our responsibilities outweighed desires

i don't like the kisses you gently placed on my forehead
right below my hairline
the way even though i was ill and contagious

you begged for a way to make me shine

all these things i really don't like
they replay in my brain
a record i just flip back and forth
waiting for the day

do i snap it in half over my knee?
or do i throw it in a fit of rage?
or do i return it to its rightful place
tucked back safely, until maybe again one day

i really don't believe in liking things
when it comes to you, it's not enough
i never really like many things, simply put
liking just isn't you,
you are love

pt. 2

i need you more than you need me
a necessary part, macaroni to cheese
front porches, ice cold sweet tea
cowboy hats, you're Tennessee
i need you more than you need me

i need you more than you need me
a necessary part, almost a comedy
flock of sheep, border collie
christmas mistletoe, holly
i need you more, by gosh by golly

i need you more than you need me
a necessary part to this book of poetry
honey for the honey bee
clownfish, my anemone
i need you more than you need me

i need you more than you need me
a necessary part, a dog to a flea
a plover, crocodile's teeth
a flower to that honey bee
i need you more than you need me

replay

i would let you hurt me
so many times
cause i know you didn't want this
and I'm the one who lied
because i would push back all my hope
just to look into your eyes
and i would let you hurt me
a hundred thousand times...

a fix

on the sweet beginner's bliss
do you ever rewind, look back
the deep and pure conversations
the instantaneous laughs
or do you just replay the crazy at the end
seeing only the girl who longed for more
more than you stated you wished for
something beautiful, though, that's for damn sure
sitting across wooden tables and booths
you order a drink, maybe even two
me too shy at first
just to let loose
you find it endearing and maybe a little cute
you brushing my cheek and
laying kisses on my forehead
trying to kiss me while i drive
as if it were worth it to wind up dead
if just one last kiss could be had
we'll never know, this beaten path
because all you'll look back on
is a girl who wanted something
something we could never really have
though as serene as it once was
it turned into this bitter mess

where i fight this uphill battle
my feelings, i'm sorry i can't help but confess
and it may be so utterly crazy to you
but if you really don't know
i don't believe you're perfect, no
but all the imperfections i loved to get to know
and there was nothing all that bad
about loving you the was i did
except for the part where it got too real
and like a child in play, you hid
games and my heart
never that good of a mix
but it was never your heart
so no, i wouldn't dare expect you to fix.

release

i loosen my grip
it's undeniably the most formidable thing i've done
surgeries, house fires, car accidents
this is number one
because pain in my heart and head combined
only get deeper as i try to fight
but i'm giving up
my eyes have been blackened for too long, swollen shut
my limbs keep snapping
twisting, fractured
nothing left of me
but traces of pain endured
but all at my own hand
i will never blame you
you tied the laces
but i wore the shoes
tripping and falling
you tied them too loose
tied them together
just like i did the noose
and i did this to myself
and i'd do it all again
because if i don't let go of you now
i fear there'd never be any end

i won't keep begging
try my best not to annoy
for this is hard enough
though in presence, so much joy
whiplash, broken necks
i can't help but keep turning
there will always be a light
inside of me, for you, burning

the well

hey... it's me again
unless you forgot
but how could i forget you
it's like you're a never ending thought
a run-on sentence, casually trickled
with semi-colons, commas, hyphens
the letters on the pages disappear
bringing the white back all its lightness
nightmare may be harsh
but you realize it's true
you made things seem so perfect
then disappeared right into the blue
i laugh it off, you gave us plans
you told me all these things and then
leaving was the only plan, goodbye
only "goodbye" was never mentioned in the end.

hey, it's me again
but i'm just a pretty face
you treated like your lover once
then said "woah slow down the pace"
but i can't take back my feelings
after already leaping, i fall
i got half way down that well

then that well turned into a hall
i hit my head against the floor
and black out, momentarily
then i pick myself back up again
ignore the dizziness, temporarily
i dust myself off
try to cover up the bruises
but there's blood and several nasty bumps
anywhere your lips brushed kisses
i look in all directions
more directions than one can count
but which way was i supposed to go
i need the most efficient route
i start to panic as you've become
the worst type of drug
the push and the pull, i start hallucinating
now look, i'm standing on a rug
and we all know what happens
when you stand on top of a rug
my feet come out from under me
in a swift, abrupt tug
so swift, i never saw it coming
even though... you've done this before
back to being that same old drug
manipulative to the core
so i yell and i scream
i look down and i think i've scraped my knees

but when i try to reach you after hurting me so bad
"i hope you're having a lovely day"
showing you kindness makes me sad
i've fallen, i've blacked out, i've panicked, now i'm
bruised
but you just sit there on your throne
unaware you've made me used
like a dirty shred of napkin
or a bottle or a glass
brushed away from a table where you feast
on broken people at last.

but hey, it's me again,
i've already forgotten, i'd let you come back
it's been so long now though
maybe i'm just a memory that you lack
like a fallen off button
string that's frayed, a remnant
of all those useless words
all a part of the enchantment
well, useless might be harsh
but one day maybe I'll be heard
one day i can tell you all my falls and woes
when you... were just a coward

hey, it's me again,
wondering how someone so seemingly fragile

can live so high while i'm in agony
the mental shown on skin, but you're casual
if you felt suffocated, i'm sorry
but i really never tried to be
i backed off so much you never even really
got to know the truest me
maybe that was why, but you said you didn't want this
confused as hell, while bruised as well
after all, you didn't want this.

hey it's me, i see you
high and mighty on that throne, you shine
i loved you even though, i know
you were never even mine
i can't resist, i don't love softly
it's never really been my strong suit
i go and sink so deeply
it's my own fault but i'll still always do it
but this one, this one is not my fault
no matter which way you try to throw it
you manipulate with your words and lines
then make me feel inadequate
is this how all the rest have felt,
everyone singing along to your tune?
how many others have there been?
do you just make everyone swoon?
there's holes dug all around me

i've seen this same image before
every well you've ever built
as i peer down all i see...
the floor

sleepless

with the lack of a "goodnight"
how could my mind begin to dream?
new worlds can't be made from no foundation, can they?
maybe you imagine differently, it would seem

with the absence of "sleep well"
how could sleeping actually feel like rest?
when my mind runs miles, marathons along the lining of
my pillowcase
this I can truly atest

a shortage, a desperately low supply of "sweet dreams"
would cause a mind to seldom be at this thing that we
call ease
it's true, this mind would rather rest right along side
yours, intertwining
but with the distance between our bodies, a simple lit
screen would appease

"don't let the bed bugs bite" would be too unadorned
it's likely that's the reason you're unable to be bothered
extravagant is never needed, not necessary in the least
but a simple "goodnight" from you, I would be truly
honored

off-record

i'm tired of watching comedies
because you made me laugh the most
and you left with such a swiftness
my laugh seemed to follow you like a host
you took it on a journey
touring room after room after room
from impersonations and loud outbursts
all your comedy i would consume
i would never ever tire
of the pain within my cheeks
i'm sure they never lacked of color
just like strain in my obliques
the way i laughed was priceless
you couldn't buy it from a store
but my laughter never could compare
to that face i did grow to adore
you see, your face is not one that gets forgotten
not easily, that is
getting lost in your eyes
is a feeling i will always come to miss
don't make me say it louder
i miss you, that's all
you seem just fine without me
just leave my laughter down the hall

i'll get up to reclaim it eventually
but for now i'll lie in wait
maybe one day you'll come back
don't forget you planned that date
you seemed so adamant
so ready to repeat that sound
like a roadtrip song worth replaying
a tape you love to have rewound
a record you never flip
just replacing the needle time and time again
but for some reason you removed that record
and never actually play it back in the end

the flower

i can't wait any longer
i'm sorry but it's true
i've waited long enough to know
the story won't end with you
it's disappointing and heartbreaking
we've had a sensational time
but i can't keep just sitting here
trying to define
wondering when you'll write me back
or if in reality we would be
i wanted you
and even though you said
you never wanted me
it never seemed to feel that way
you told fairytales of us
you wined me and you dined me
and you made me feel
...not loved
you see, love wasn't what you wished for
but i could love you in all the best ways
i want to know your darkest truths
and your foremost memories
all i wanted was to sing your praise
i'd do it all the time

i'd love you morning, noon and night
absent never from my mind
this reigns true now even though
it's not reciprocated
forgive me, please, i'm fully aware
but you clearly were elated
you couldn't hide your expression of joy
when we would share a room
i knew it from the day we met
i could feel a flower bloom
and i know you felt it too
but you took that flower far away
you hit it from the sun
you hit it, i think you were scared
that flower could be the most beautiful one
it's okay, i know
you made your intentions clear
you never wanted me, not at all
definitely not here
we've had a sensational time
but i can't keep patiently dwelling here
waiting
wondering
wading
for you to someday cast a line
cause i'll bite
but i'll keep swimming for now

cause i know you won't dare put up the fight
and it's fine, i know, i'm so aware
your intentions crystal, fully clear
only i already had the itch, the bite
and only your love held the cure

shortness of life

life is too short
to not love loudly
to not admit we have a crush for the sake of losing
someone we've wanted so badly
to act like nothing is there when sparks have flown
to not embrace the feelings
to act like we don't care
to act like nothing... is there
life is far too short to sit here and wait
when you've said you wanted nothing
to sit here and wait
to see that you just meant with me
life is far too short to watch you from afar
and wonder if you really ever meant words you spoke
after a night at the bar
life is far too short
to simply watch so i will act
i will tell you my true feelings and not stop until my
lungs collapse
because i can feel myself falling more and more and yet
you *push*
but life is to short to try to pull myself back
when every time you push
you build a wall i cannot crack

life is too short
so let me let you go but you won't
you still toss out crumbs of sweet nothings my way
let me let you go but you won't
and at the end of the day
it's my fault
because life is too short
but i can't let you go
because i can't tell you how i feel about that certain look
you give with the raise of a brow
and the things that you do that bring a burst of joy
through my mouth
and the ease of being myself in your presence makes me
feel like no other person has ever needed existence
you're like summer in the winter and sunshine through
the clouds
but also like a storm, when i've just gotten to the beach
and set out my towels
well life is too short
so i'll sit here and enjoy it
because life is far too short
to try to run away from it

pt. 3

i need you more than you need me
a necessary part, beauty, yes, the need to see
poetry, we need to read
energy, the need to feed
i need you way more than you need me

i need you more than you need me
a most necessary part, a beautiful dream
art, you be my gallery
art, hell, you can be da Vinci
i need you more than you need me

i need you more than you need me
the most painful part, i can't believe
oxygen, to breathe
life support, a dripping IV
i need you way more than you need me

i need you more than you need me
a necessary part, my melancholy reality
pain, therapy
illness, remedy
confusion, clarity

i need you, simple as can be

www.ingramcontent.com/pod-product-compliance
Lightning Source LLC
LaVergne TN
LVHW010021200726
843495LV00015B/1871